Real Estate Investing After the Meltdown

Real Estate Investing After the Meltdown

How to Succeed in the Upcoming Market Turmoil

Daniel J. O'Leary II

Copyright 2014 © El Paso Real Estate LLC

You may not copy, reproduce, post, or forward this document in any format.

Legal Disclaimer:

The information contained in this report was compiled and distributed in good faith but should not be considered a substitute for legal advice. The information contained in this report is meant to guide you through the investment process, but is not meant to be a comprehensive guide due to varying regulations and legal requirements in different counties and jurisdictions across the nation. You should always consult with a professional before investing in a property.

TABLE OF CONTENTS

Chapter 1 Looking Back

Hero Snow   7
The meltdown bankrupted many

Looking Forward   9
The return of the Real Estate Cycle
Market Cycles
Four challenges ahead
New Market Investor Thinking Points

Chapter 2 The New Market Investor

A Change of Perspective   12
Who is the new investor?
Where to find the money
Self directed retirement funds, Mortgage Companies,
Banks, Private Investors, Hard Money Lenders
New Market Investor Thinking Points

Chapter 3 Single Family Homes

Your Residence   18
Four things to remember when purchasing your first home
Repairs, Divorce, Death, Job Loss, Job Transfers

Chapter 4 Single Family Homes as an Investment

Strategies of the new market investor   21
The first tool for the new market investor
Analysis Tools Block

Analyzing single family homes   22
Location, Size, Neighborhood amentities, Income, Maintenance,
Management, Collection and bad debt, Replacements, Examples
Strategy Box

Chapter 5 Single Family Homes as a Business   30
Wholesale
Top five places to find great deals
Calculating the purchase price
Repairs
Calculating the purchase price

Wholesale profit
Rehabbing
Contractors
Options, wraps, and others
The blended business

Chapter 6 Multifamily Homes
Which is the better real estate investment?   40
Finding the emerging market
The niche analysis

Chapter 7 Analysis of the Multifamily
Burnt out landlords, Poor management,
Properties that need repair, Low rents, High vacancies   43
Types of properties

Analyzing the cash flow   45
Income
Market rents VS current rents

Expenses   46
Vacancies and credit loss
Management fees
Repairs and maintenance
Operating expenses
Processing the cash flow

Determining Price   47
Cash on cash return
Formula
Return on investment
Debt coverage ratio

Becoming a new market investor   50

Chapter 1
Looking Back

I hope you like change. The last ten years have certainly brought a lot of it and the next ten will bring even more.

The economic and housing meltdown of '06 and '07 turned the real estate industry up on its ear. Eight years later, we are still reeling and attempting to recover.

Many people in the industry that I knew (realtors, investors, appraisers, builders, and developers) were brought to their knees, and some ended up leaving the business.

The warning bells sounded from many sources. People had been talking about overheated markets for several years, but it's hard to hear the sirens when you are inside where the party is going on.

Hero Snow

I grew up snow skiing. I remember the excitement of waking up to a brand new "dump" of fresh powder because you knew the skiing would be great that day. We used to call it "hero snow" because the skiing was so easy on the new snow that everyone felt like a hero when they skied.

The early 2000's was like that. Everyone was a successful "investor." California had been through a long period of appreciation and many home owners found they had made over a million just in the equity of their personal residences. These new real estate millionaires were scouring the country looking to reproduce their profits. The markets were "hot" all over the country. We were seeing multiple offers on most properties. I remember doing an appraisal on a property that sold $15,000 over what it should have. When I called the agent involved, I would ask "...let me guess, it's a California buyer right?"
"Yes."
"Have they seen the property?"
"No."

"Have they been to El Paso?"
"No."
"Do they know they are paying too much?"
"Yes."

These buyers had just sold their own home for a million dollars. A house that costs $160,000 was chicken feed, and since everything looked like it would continue upwards they would make another million on the next one. Hero snow.

We bought and sold quite a few homes from these out of town investors when the market turned and they could no longer afford to carry the properties.

Everyone wanted in the game. Realtors and mortgage people had been in for a while, but all walks of life were flooding to real estate. The returns had been consistent and Wall Street was disappointing.

The meltdown bankrupted many

The bulk of these new investors are gone now. These people were buying and holding properties at prices too high, with cash flow too low to sustain itself through a market downturn.

I didn't foresee the bubble burst. I just got lucky. I was holding around 30 properties in 2005 when the appraisal business was getting really hot. I had staffing issues on the property management side and it was really a headache for me. I decided to sell the properties. I sold my last property in March of 2006, so my timing was pure luck. Had I held them onto them through the down turn, it would have most likely hurt me financially.

Recovery has been slow and *real* recovery will continue to be slow. We are seeing cities with some relief in the housing sector, but the gains are short term and will be over shadowed by the economic turmoil ahead.

The roosters will be coming home to roost, and the governments around the world are going to have to pay the price for their debt addictions. I am not a fan of listening to those who preach doom and gloom, but I see the reality of what is happening every day. I don't know how everything will play out, however, I do believe most of us are going to take a hit in our income and standard of living.

Looking Forward

The return of the Real Estate cycle

Historically, real estate went through a natural business cycle of growth and recession, as did other areas of the economy. As there had not been a real estate recession since the 80's, many people forgot what they were. We thought the Federal Government had solved the real estate cycle with its monetizing activities. Many participants in the real estate market did not factor holding onto a property through a down-market, although most have the skills and knowledge to acquire properties that will maintain themselves.

Market cycles

Real estate market cycles follow the normal supply and demand curves
(waves). When the demand for homes is high, sellers are in control and prices are rising. Developers increase their supply to take advantage of the demand. The builders and developers continue until there is an over supply. The market tips to a buyers market with too much inventory and buyers driving prices down. This is the normal cycle and is usually run in about 9 year cycles (keeping in mind that not all areas will be in the same cycle at the same time).

The new economy investor must learn to not only ride these cycles, but to thrive in them. There are strategies for each type of market and investment criteria to help ride the waves.

Four challenges ahead

The four specters haunting real estate will continue for some time. First, consumer confidence both in the economy and in the dream of home ownership is not what it used to be. Many people lost overleveraged homes and that bitterness is out there. Younger families are not buying anywhere near the rates of the past, they just don't see homeownership as viable.

The second specter is jobs. Where the jobs go, people go. Most areas of the country are not successfully creating new jobs. For real estate, it's all about jobs.

The third specter is the lending environment. What was once one of the largest industries in the US – the mortgage industry became a train wreck and getting it back on track is proving to be difficult. Lenders are skittish, it is over-regulated, and what seems like a weekly occurrence, is being assaulted with new lawsuits from the US government. In light of this environment, it is no wonder that homebuyers are finding it difficult to get loans.

The fourth specter is that the baby boomers (the largest consuming generation that drove the economic prosperity of the last 20 years) are dying. As they leave the market they are not replaced numerically with other home buyers. Areas that are unable to attract new population with jobs will have a hard time with this.

In light of the current and future economic forces, real estate will have a somewhat difficult pull in the next ten years. It will, however, fair much better than most other industries as the economics and landscape will be changing across all sectors. The investor with the foresight and skills to properly analyze a property will find huge opportunities.

So what is the new perspective and how will the savvy new market investor deal with the uncertainty of the coming years? First of all, the successful investor will be picky about where he or she invests or what type of property they invest in. They will build in their profits before they purchase. They will insure sufficient cash flow to whether down turns and vacancies. These tactics will help to minimize risk, and by utilizing the tax benefits of real estate, they will help to maximize wealth building.

In the years ahead, many of us will be turning to real estate as it will be a more secure and manageable income stream. Some will seek it for retirement, and some for vocation. Real estate will weather fairly well, but it must be done right. The old method of throwing mud up on the wall and seeing what sticks, won't work. Not all properties will do well. Not all prices are OK. To succeed in the coming decade, the investor must have a new focus with new tools, to become a "New Market" investor.

New Market Investor Thinking Points

1. The next 10 years will most likely be full of economic turmoil.
2. Investors will enter the market as secondary income becomes necessary.
3. Real Estate can do well.
4. New tools and analysis are necessary, as not all properties and not all prices will give a return.

Chapter 2
The New Market Investor

A change of perspective

The first thing necessary to change for the successful investor in the new market is a change of perspective. We have all been taught to buy low and sell high to make a profit. As a society, however, we are generally convinced to doing the exact opposite.

Take stocks for instance, most people buy stocks when the market is booming and they end up plummeting in a market crash. Who is making money here? The institutional players and the contrarians are the ones who benefit.

Warren Buffett, the famous investor, says to "be fearful when others are greedy and greedy when others are fearful". Interesting.

Does this apply to real estate? When the news media says that real estate is booming, your cousin just made money, and he urges you to get on board, where do you think the market is at that time? That's right, it is at a peak. If you buy at current prices, when the market turns down, you can lose equity. So in essence, following public opinion, we actually buy high and sell low.

I call this type of investing "speculation." Buying at market value and hoping that prices go up is somewhat of a fool's game and it is the reason why so many people are disillusioned with Wall Street.

There is a better way. The economic turmoil of the next ten years will require a more predictable investing approach. The successful investor is one who makes their money when they buy the property. Not when the market goes up. The investor who learns to make arrangements for their profits when they purchase has a more diverse skill set that can be utilized in either a rising or declining market.

To successfully succeed in the new economics, the savvy investor will need the foresight and skills to analyze and price a property in

such a way as to insure both profit and the ability for the property to carry itself in a downturn.
This takes a little more knowledge, a little more skill, and a lot more work. That's why very few will do it and a very few will make tons of money.

Who is the new investor?

The old model of job security and retirement, either from a company or the government, has been an illusion for a while. This will become more evident as entitlement programs continue to be slashed. The worker as a fee agent will become better understood and will be embraced as the savvy take control of their destinies.

Outsourcing to other countries will continue, and not just for better wages, but for a better educated employee. The US has completely messed up its' education system.

The current generation is showing more entrepreneurial spirit than any generation before. This is most likely because of the hard facts of the job market have given them no choice. These new business minded people are realizing that the internet has given them the ability to do what only large retailers could do in the past. They can sell. The retail middle man is taking a hit right now and mom and pop are stepping in and learning to make money. These new business savvy entrepreneurs will have the knowledge and drive to become the next wave of real estate fortune hunters.

As big, if not bigger, than the young entrepreneurs are the retiring boomers and echo boomers. Left with raided pensions that don't exist and social security that does not support retirement, this group will be looking for work and fulfillment. Many will find real estate a perfect fit for semi-retirement.

Whether full or part time, real estate investing can be flexible enough to have a strong appeal to those taking control of their professional and financial future. As Wall Street, corporate America, and big government continue to reveal how flawed they are, many will find a great fit here. It will, however, require hard work and knowledge.

Were to find the money

Typically, real estate investing requires money. Most investing is some combination of the investor's funds and a loan. Some deal structures utilize all other people's money which we will look at shortly.

Personal funds are the first source to consider as it is easy to find. You know right where it is and you have control over it. The down side to this source of money is that it is normally limited. After the initial purchases and the funds are used up it can take some time to replenish. This is where many investors begin to learn how to find other sources of capital for investing. Before taking about those sources, lets look at an often over looked source of funds.

Self directed retirement funds

Many people have pensions or 401K plans from their employer. Most of us have been trained (by the people who charge to manage these funds) that they must be invested in Wall Street products. These portfolios have been traditionally invested in stocks and bonds, but the stock market crash and the poor returns have left most investors disillusioned with the stock market.

Retirement accounts can be self managed, and real estate can be bought inside of a 401K or pension. When considering the tax free growth inside most of these plans, the ability to purchase real estate, enjoy tax free cash flow and appreciation can be an exiting new concept to help supercharge retirement planning.

The next area to look at is friends and family. Once again close at hand, easy to find but not always easy to convince. Some of the worst partnerships are with friends and family because of the emotions that arise regarding money that will sometimes supersede good business decisions. However, many investors I know have partnerships with family and friends in properties.

Mortgage companies

Mortgage lenders are the major players in the 1 to 4 family markets. In the past, an investor could get a loan of up to 95% of the price of the property. Most loans currently are in the 80% to 90% range with closing costs of around 3%. A loan of 80% would require a 20% down payment, so a $300,000 property would require a $60,000 down payment with around $9,000 in closing costs, making acquisition costs right at $69,000.

Banks

Banks and insurance companies are the traditional source of funds for purchases of multifamily properties above 4 units, with insurance companies usually only interested in larger loans. Loan to values are typically 70% to 80%.

Private investors

Many individuals like investing in real estate but don't want the hassle of managing the property. This is very easily accomplished by lending for the purchaser. The private lender gets an investment secured by the property, a guaranteed return higher than securities, no tenants or toilets, and the investor gets the money for the transaction.

Hard money lenders

These loans are typically for a shorter duration, utilized for bridging a rehab or remodel and sale. The rates and terms of these loans are typically higher so use of this source should be high profit fast concluding transactions. Typical fees in these transactions are 3 to 5 points (or percentage points) paid up front in addition to typical closing costs with rates from 9% to 13%. Loan to value is typically 60% to 70%.

There are three basic ways to approach investing, as the single investor – doing it all on their own, as a group with each member performing in the area of their strengths, and in a syndication, with a lead investor utilizing their experience and managing the investment. Let's look at all three.

As a single investor, the benefit of this method is that of retaining control of all decisions and the ability to learn all aspects of the process. In the group or syndication, many decisions will me made by other people, and although often, more heads are better than one, some people don't see things that way.

Another advantage is the ability to experience the various aspects of the investment process. You learn to analyze the property through acquisition, learning about maintenance, leasing, tenant relations, legal issues, and accounting. There are a myriad of disciplines that will require the single investor to grow in knowledge and experience. Investors come to realize that this is a team activity and your success in investing will be a function of the quality of the team you put together. Working relationships with Realtors, Contractors, Inspectors, Appraisers, Property Managers, Accountants, and Attorneys are all necessary for successful investing. Who is on your team?

Often in a team, a group will form with one or more people with the skills noted above. Often one person will be good at finding the properties, another at repair and maintenance, and another at management. These partnerships can help to make the process flow when the group works well together, but can also become difficult when one or more members become unhappy.

The syndication has the benefit of the lead investor performing the function of organizing the investment and supervising all property management and maintenance, and giving the other investors a passive role in the process. Most entities will also protect the other investors from legal issues which help to manage an investor's risk. This is a very good scenario for the investor who is busy with other endeavors.

New Market Investor Thinking Points

1. Investor must move from speculator, to Investor.
2. Investor makes arrangement for their profit when they buy, not by praying that prices go up.
3. There are many sources of funds, not only traditional sources, but investing groups, syndications, and retirement funds.

Chapter 3
Single Family Homes

Your residence

Let's begin by looking at the home that you live in. The questions are, "Is it an asset? Is it an investment?" It most likely has some attributes of each of those, however, this can be argued. Robert Kiyosaki, the famous investor, makes the argument that maybe the home that you live in is not in fact an asset. As he defines it, an asset must bring in cash flow and require a minimum amount of participation.

I am not sure if I totally agree with his perspective. I have seen so many people develop more wealth in their personal residences than in any other endeavor. Therefore, I do believe that your personal residence is a good investment.

As real estate investors, it is in fact our goal to create cash flow. This is the reason why we invest. From that standpoint, the argument could be made that your individual home is not necessarily an asset. It's generally not a cash producing asset for most of us.

Another dynamic of the homes we live in is the quality of life issue. We often desire features and amenities beyond what would normally be put in the home. I can understand this, and forgive the mistakes we make on our personal homes in terms of over-improving them. However, I would be remiss not to mention how frequently I am in the home of a shocked homeowner who can't believe that the $75,000 that they spent "pimping" out their 1,200 sq ft starter home doesn't add $75,000 of value. In the marketplace, cost very seldom equals value.

My rule of thumb here is to keep a close eye on the homes in your neighborhood and don't improve beyond what is typical. Money spent beyond that point should be considered a luxury and money possibly never regained.

If you are looking at buying your first home, I would recommend considering two things beyond whether you will like living in the house or not. First, will the house perform well as an investment? Second, will it rent well if and when you are in a position to move up?

Here are four things to remember when purchasing your first home.

1. Remember to buy with the prospect of reselling the home. What type of home sells best and easiest in the market?
2. Don't over improve your home or buy a home too large for the area, resale and cost recovery gets difficult.
3. Buy with your first rental in mind. The home you are buying may end up being your first rental property, does it fit the market?
4. Be ready to separate yourself emotionally from the home if you put in into service as a rental.

We will talk more about all these issues in later chapters. As to the performance of the home as an investment, I will discuss this in the next few chapters. This will include neighborhood, age, market fit, and other topics to help zero in on the issues that help to maximize demand and value for a house. We will also talk about successful renting. Even if you are only looking at purchasing your first home, there should be value there for you.

One important strategy is to remember that the primary residence that you have lived in for 2 years can be sold free from capitol gains tax. So effectively, if you sold the home you lived in every two years or so your profits are tax free. A remodel in an area with upper value mobility can be a very nice play.

The smart home buyer will try to buy a property with some type of "value play."

- Does the home need work that if corrected will bring more money than the cost to correct? This is a very tricky one – my experience from the appraisal side of the business is that cost does not equal value, and usually people overestimate the value that a repair will bring. Actually most repairs solve problems that only bring the property up to the values of the other homes in the neighborhood. If a property needs repair be sure that the discount you pay on the property is sufficient to recoup the cost and your time.

- Divorce. This extremely traumatic experience will cause huge changes in the economic out look for everyone. Often the home will be awarded to one or the other spouse, but often times that spouse can not afford to keep and maintain the home.

- Death. Heirs are often times unequipped to deal with the inheritance of a home. We have purchased many homes from relative in other cities who just cant take the time to deal with an inherited property.

- Job Loss. Loss of income certainly affects the ability to keep a property. Bing the right person at the right time to help the family out of a crisis can create a value play.

- Job Transfers. Most Job offers don't afford 6 months to a year for the employee to wrap up affairs in another city. Usually they want the person now. We frequently are dealing with a spouse who is vary ready to join their family in the new city and to get rid of the burden of two payments.

There are a multitude of other scenarios where there is the ability to create value in the purchase because a home has become a burden. One of the keys to being good at putting deals together is to learn to listen to what the underlying problems are and to find solutions.

Chapter 4
Single Family Homes as an Investment

Strategies of the new market investor

Single family homes or (SFR – single family residences to save trees) can be purchased for two types of outcomes. First, to "buy and hold," or to rent, where the tenant pays the underlying loan and equity is created. This "buy and hold" is a long term strategy and sometimes requires parking cash in properties.

Secondly for short term cash flow, purchase and wholesale to other investors or to fix and flip (other variations will be discussed later). This activity is more in line with normal business models that require the activity to generate immediate profits.

I meet many frustrated investors who attempt to turn the "buy and hold" strategy into a business and find it too slow or cash intensive. Even if the investor becomes skilled at purchasing using their own money, they tend to find the properties do need some investment in maintenance and the monthly cash flow isn't large. It takes quite a few properties initially to generate enough cash flow to run a business.

Some investors usually graduate to the business model to help support the activities of the first model. For some, however, the first model fits their bill entirely and is all the activity they need. I do suggest for those who are strictly "Buy and Hold" to consider a technique called amortizing the debt.

The first tool for the new market investor

Almost the exact opposite of high leverage (more leverage = more risk) this technique accelerates the pay off of the property. By making extra payments into the initial property rather than purchasing another, using both the rent from the tenant, and additional investment the property is paid off as quickly as possible. The next property is then purchased and the income from the first and second property plus additional investment into the second property pays off the second even faster. Then onto the third, and so forth.

One of the major benefits for the new market investor is a lot less risk, holding free and clear properties is a lot easier in a slow market where it may be hard to find a tenant. If there is no payment on the mortgage an empty house doesn't hurt as much..

Also, this method can get you to large monthly cash flow faster. Having 5 to 10 properties free and clear is a retirement goal of many people I consult with.

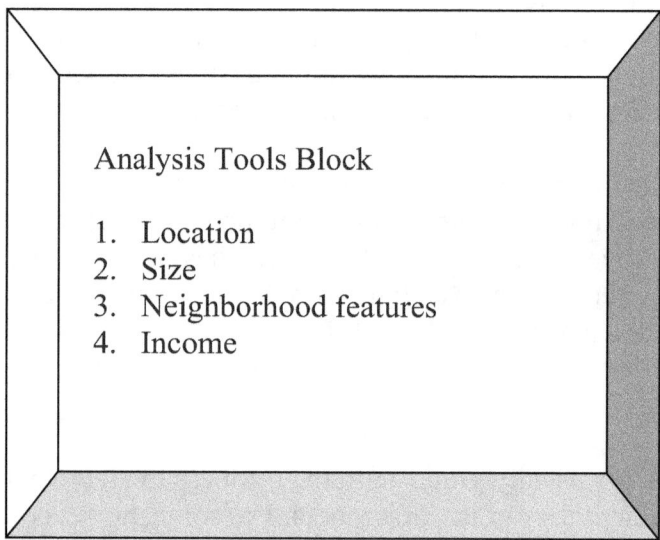

Analyzing single family homes

Most first time single family investors become so by default. They end up with too many homes through marriage, inheritance, etc. Not so much by design but by default they are having a hard time selling so they decide to try their hand at landlording. A large percentage of these landlords are unprepared for the discipline and negotiation of dealing with a tenant. We have run into countless situations where a tenant is 8 or ore months back on rent.

It starts out fairly harmless. We all know what it is like to have more month than money. A person goes down the list trying to find who they can put off. Then there is the story to the landlord about the job or whatever and we will catch it up real soon. This produces the first twinge of fear for the new landlord as they realize that they will be making the payment on the property instead of the tenant. Next month is another story and promises more adamantly made, maybe even a partial payment made. It goes bad fast from there. The tenant begins dodging, the landlord feels invested, and looks back at the $3,000 that the tenant owes, and is afraid to throw them out and loose all the money.

One of our favorite places to buy properties is at the Justice of the Peace court in possession suits. These "Burned out Landlords" are highly motivated to get rid of the properties that have been causing them to lose sleep for the last 6 months as well as a good portion of their savings.

There are two things that should be done to prevent property train wrecks. We need better management systems (we will look at these later in the chapter) and better property selection criteria. Choosing the right property is not in our control when we inherit, or a home we have lived in becomes a rental, but becomes critical to our return and profit when buying investment homes.

Better understanding of how a property will perform is key to riding out fluctuations in the economy and real estate markets. The new market investor will attempt to take out as much market risk as possible by ensuring a sound investment analysis of the properties considered. So what analysis tools should the investor use to help deal with these issues?

Location

The one thing that affect values and rental demand more than any other is in fact location, location, location.

Neighborhood characteristics affect who wants to live in an area. Things like schools, proximity to shopping and work affect demand.

Knowing where people want to live and projecting where demand will be in the next 10 years will pay off big for the investor. Underlying social and economic factors affect demand and therefore price. It is somewhat easy to see these factors change as you drive through areas. Homes will go from smaller to larger, newer to older, average quality to better, and well kept to neglected.

Neighborhoods go through normal life cycles. The first is the new cycle which usually lasts around 10 to 15 years and this is where the property appreciation occurs. The second is that of maturity, another 10 to 15 year cycle with fairly flat appreciation. This is followed by a period of decline where demand wanes and values will erode. The forth stage is renewal. It is hard to project if and when this stage will occur, families are moving back into the neighborhood, and the properties are being updated.

There are specific investment strategies that work in each cycle, but to maximize success and return, the safest cycle to be in is the first, properties under 20 years old, where demand is highest.

Size

I know some investors who prefer larger move up homes as they feel that they attract a more financially sound tenant. I believe that this can be true but it can also make it harder to find a tenant. I tend to prefer to invest in the heart of the market, the range that has the most renters and the most demand. The average sales price in a market represents the most demand. In my market, that is around $150,000 and about 1700 square feet. I prefer to stay above 1400 square feet as below that the homes are slightly small for some families. 1800 to 2500 square feet is a great size range. At 1800 square feet the second living area has made its appearance and overall room sizes just feel better. 1800 square foot plus homes rent and sell faster.

Neighborhood amenities

To appeal to the broadest market, a neighborhood needs good features. What are these features? Some call them infrastructure, but it is the social needs of the neighborhood such as schools and parks. Shopping, public transportation, proximity to work and freeways, will be available in a good neighborhood.

These come together to help make up the aesthetics of the neighborhood. There is an overall feel for a good neighborhood. Walk neighborhoods you are interested in after the families are home in the evening. You will get a great feel for the type of people in the neighborhood. Are the properties well kept or are there weeds growing through the cars parked in the yards? Too many rentals in an area detract from the desirability. If you are not comfortable walking the area or would not want to live there, is it where you should be investing?

Income

My favorite topic - Income. To get a point a cross I will tell the story of an "old school" investor I know G. (Gone) Broke (you guessed it the story is not flattering so no real names) got a book about building a real estate rental empire using no money down techniques. One of the techniques was to take over the payments on the properties (not judging this technique, we do this sometimes but see warnings below). Gone found it fairly easy to find these properties and when he could rent it out for the mortgage payment he took the property. It did not take long before Mr. Broke had over 40 of these properties in portfolio. One day he noticed the repair calls had started to pile up. A roof repair here, AC repairs all over, several water heaters to replace, a stove out there. Cash flow was getting hit. The market turned down and the rental cycle started, people were moving out of some of the properties and it was taking several months to replace the tenants. Mr. Broke suddenly was making quit a few mortgage payments out of his own pocket. And then he couldn't make some of the payments. The calls from the old owners who he had promised he would make the payments on their loans started, then the calls from the banks calling the loans due started, and then the calls from the attorneys started. Mr. Broke made it out but not with any assets. I have known some to get caught in this trap and actually serve time for fraud. If you promise someone you will do something and you don't do it there can be trouble.

So what did Mr. G. Broke do wrong? He bought properties that weren't cash flowing and he bought too many of them. (He also assumed risk for someone else that he was unable to cover.)

The decade before us will have many ups and downs across many markets, real estate included so the successful investor must be prepared to weather various types of storms. Cash flow is your friend in tough times. You need enough cash flow in your properties to cover more than just the rent. There are many other expenses in a property that must be taken into account.

Maintenance

Landscaping, trash removal, snow removal, plumbing problems, broken windows, pest control, Heat and AC service. These must all be projected and accounted for.

Management

Many investors don't account for management of their properties. Since many manage their properties themselves they don't take into account the cost of management. The Commercial Real Estate Designation CCIM members use an operating analysis form called an APOD (annual property operating data) that projects cash flows from a property for 5 years. One of the first items listed on this form is management expenses. When looking at large projects, management expenses are always taken into consideration. The savvy investor knows the value of the time it takes to run a property and will calculate this expense, usually 10%.

Collection and bad debt

Unless all your tenants are perfect (really?) you will have expenses involved in debt collection. Industry standards are 3% to 5%.

Replacements

True expenses on a single-family property go well beyond just normal cleaning, painting, and fixing the toilets. You're going to have some of those expenses as well as labor and up keep on the property. But the true expenses of a property are also in what you would call the depreciable items or the short lived items. You know, different portions and structures in the property have age lives that differ from the overall life of the property. Typically homes will last 90 some years, depending on the construction and whether they're kept up. But that doesn't mean that all the parts of the house will last those 90 years.

One of the shortest lived items obviously in a house would be paint. Paint might last four or five years depending upon wear and tear, and whether or not there are children. Children and pets can be real tough on all those surfaces. Carpet in a home has a fairly short lifespan also. You might be doing very well to get five or six years out of carpet in a home with heavy traffic. So every five or six years that carpet has to be replaced. Appliances, water heaters, furnaces all have an eight to ten year life span. You also need to take into consideration some of the major structures like the roof. Depending upon the type of roof, and upon the part of the country that you're in, you might do well at a 10 or 15 year lifespan on a shingle or tile roof.

This is where many first time investors can get into trouble. A couple of ill timed repairs, a roof leak, or a water heater replacement that someone was not prepared for can really hurt financially. I have seen situations where property owners flat could not afford their repairs, lose their tenants, and without the rent, lose the property.

Better outcomes require better analysis. What most people don't do is take into account that they're going to have those types of expenses. The analysis takes the total or the remaining life (estimate of how many years left before replacing). For example, we take the cost of the new roof and we divide it by the remaining life years and we get an approximate yearly figure. We divide that by 12 and we get a figure that effectively should be going into a sinking fund monthly. We add all these expenses and then we compare it to the revenue so we get a more realistic view of this. Here is a list of items with typical age lives (your area will vary as per weather etc.).

Roof - 20 years
Exterior paint - 10 years
Interior paint - 5 years
Carpet - 7 years
Water heater - 10 years
Furnace - 15 years
AC - 15 years
Range - 10 Years

Let's look at an example:

Item cost	Cost	Remaining Life	Monthly
Roof	$7,000	15 Years	$38.89
Exterior Paint	$2,000	8 Years	$20.83
Interior Paint	$2,000	5 Years	$33.33
Carpet	$3,000	5 Years	$50.00
Water Heater	$800	6 Years	$11.11
Furnace	$1,000	12 Years	$6.42
AC	$4,000	12 Years	$27.78
Range	$600	8 Years	$6.25
Total:	$20,400		$195.14

So what we see is that over the next 5 to 15 years we will have $20,400 of expenses on the property and that equates to $195.14 every month. The method of calculating cash flow by subtracting the mortgage from the rent to estimate cash flow is hugely underestimating the reality of the investment. This is one of the main reasons so many single family investors don't make money on their investments.

Paying too much for properties, and making up the cash flow might work out if you are certain for double digit appreciation, but this kind of crap shoot speculation will catch many investors in the years ahead, as the market just doesn't produce those kinds of returns in a turbulent market.

Strategy box
1. Buy and hold
2. Quick turn
3. Blend
4. Amortize the debt

Chapter 5
Single Family Homes as a Business

Unless you have a large source of money at your disposal, either from inheritance, another business, or a strong financial partner, the money to fund the real estate that you buy and hold must come from somewhere. Although it is somewhat fairly easy to buy properties without using money, at some point they will require repairs or mortgage payments. The good news is that there are aspects of the real estate business beyond just the buy and hold strategy that will generate the immediate cash flow needed. These activities take real estate beyond just the investing for retirement type activity and move it into what could be considered an extremely profitable business.

These activities include wholesaling properties, options, wraps, and rehabbing properties. There are other strategies available to the experienced investor which are usually spin offs or blends of these main three.

Wholesaling

This strategy is the fastest with the least amount of risk of any of the strategies. It doesn't require any money or loans. This is where I suggest most beginning investors start.

Wholesaling is finding a property, getting it under contract at a price that would appeal to other investors and then selling it. In this strategy we are not making repairs on the property, we are selling it just as it is. Most wholesalers usually don't even take title or close on the property. They effectively sell their contract and the new investor closes with the seller.

This activity can give the new investor a great feel for the market very quickly as other investors will let them know of desirable areas and where they would need to price to purchase. If you are over valuing properties or paying too much, the other investors will quickly let you know.

Finding the properties

In reality we are not looking for particular properties although they must fit our guidelines but we are looking for a seller with a problem. We must buy these properties in such a way that we can sell them and make money. Our goal on a wholesale deal is usually $5,000 to $10,000. Most of these properties also need work, so as we will see shortly, these properties must be purchased at a discount from market value.

There are lots of reasons why a seller would sell for less than market value. These properties have usually fallen into disrepair and sometimes the owners don't have the money, time, or energy to do the repairs. Some owners have received houses as an inheritance and live in another part of the country and traveling to repair and then sell is too much of a burden. Sometimes people get themselves into financial trouble and need money fast, to sell on the market often takes 6 months to a year and they don't have that kind of time. Sometimes the house itself is the problem where they have lost a job and can no longer make payments. So it really is all about locating people with problems and helping to find solutions. I don't suggest you spend much time with people without problems, trying to talk them into selling at a discount, it is a waste of everyone's time.

So where to we find the good deals? Here are our top five places to find great deals.

One: Realtors
If you don't already have a good relationship with a Realtor, find one that understands you are looking for a great deal. They can get you lists from their MLS on Short Sales, Bank Foreclosures, Corporate owned properties, and motivated sellers.   Sort the list by price per sq ft and the better deals will be on top.

Two: Vacants
This is the "Gum Shoe" or Detective strategy. Cruise the neighborhood you are interested in looking for vacant properties. Once you get good at this it is amazing how easy they are to spot. It starts with the over grown condition of the yard, then the eyes go to

the general non lived in appearance, no hoses, toys etc. Next, notice the windows and that you can see all the way through the property. I had my daughters trained to spot them and I would give them a dollar for each one found. It became a game to them, and they would have a ball driving through the neighborhoods. Hint: try to always drive a different way wherever you go.

Three: Auctions

Here in El Paso, the Sheriffs sale for foreclosures is the first Tuesday of every month. There are deals here but you have to know what you are doing. This method is really for the experienced investor. It is a cash sale with no way of previewing the property so it is easy to get surprised with problem properties. I would warn most people away from buying this way, you will know when you are ready.

Four: Investors

People who are constantly marketing properties usually have several for sale at good prices. Call the people with the "I buy houses" signs and see what they have.

Five: Housing Court

Find out when the Justice of the Peace is having their suits for possession and the city is fining landlords and condemning properties. These are not the same place and time but essentially the same technique. Here you find owners who are really tired of their properties. Hand them a card and tell them you would be interested in buying.

Calculating the purchase price

We have found our first potential wholesale deal from a seller who just needs rid of the property. Here is the way to calculate the offer price. First we must know what the property would sell for after repairs are done and secondly what the repairs are. Keep in mind that we are looking to sell to other investors so we must calculate a price that will allow us to make a little money and the purchasing investor to make their reasonable profit.

Here is the formula for calculating your offer.
((ARV) X 70% - Repairs)) – WS Profit = Max Offer.

>ARV is the value of the property after repaired
>70% represents profit and carry.
>Repairs work to be done
>WS Profit= Wholesale profit
>Max Offer = Max you can pay and make money.

ARV – After Repaired Value
What are homes selling for in the area? A relationship with a good Realtor or Appraiser will serve you here. Comparable sales are the key with a caution about using Zillow or Trulia. Their values typically are inflated as they are using modeling that includes too many samples. Your comps should be similar in size, location, and quality. Drive the comps and you will know which ones are not similar.

70% Profit Multiplier represents 30% profit and carry.
In the 30% is 15% profit target, all businesses need to make a profit and 15% is typical for this type of business. Most investors and builders will shoot for 15% and end up around 12%. The other 15% is closing costs. There are closing costs when you buy and closing costs when you sell. Also included are holding costs, costs for the money. So essentially you are offering 70 cents on the dollar minus repairs minus your profit.

Repairs

If you are not familiar with the cost of repairs and construction, Home Depot and Lowes have several classes and the prices are all out on the floor. I like to build a spread sheet to quickly calculate the repairs while in a property. I will have it on my tablet and enter data as we go through. Some people get too caught up in the estimating and get on the floor and measure the carpet area and linier feet for cabinets. These are usually beginners. The trick is to find short cuts as soon as possible. For instance, knowing the square foot of a property and estimating what percent is carpet will suffice. I know investors who can walk through a property and based on the major categories will estimate in $5,000 chunks. Just paint and carpet: $5,000, kitchen and baths: $10,000, roof: $15,000, etc. This typically will serve a wholesaler with experience. If we are rehabbing we break it out a little more.

Wholesale profit

We generally make between $5,000 and $10,000 on a wholesale deal. It's a matter of working the numbers in. You must make arrangements for your profits as you don't want to be trying to sell a wholesale deal on the "greater fool theory". That theory is that you hope you will find a bigger fool than you to pay more than they should. Experienced investors learn early that they can't pay too much and make a profit, and if you are hoping to find an inexperienced investor to pay more that they should this will be the only property you can sell them because they will not be in business long. Your goal is to get a great working relationship with all the investors in your area.

For example:
ARV = $100,000. Repairs = $15,000.
$100,000 X 70% = $70,000
$70,000 - $15,000 = $55,000
$55,000 - $5,000 = $50,000 Max Offer
Suggested initial offer = $47,000.

Purchasing a property at $47,000 when its value could be $100,000 once $15,000 worth of repairs were made, represents quite a bit of money. So you can see that this requires a problem property. You typically won't talk someone who has the time and resources into this type of transaction, they will do the repairs and make the profit themselves. You are looking for someone who is motivated and the property represents a problem that you can solve. They are out there. We typically find 2 to 3 of these every month, some we keep to rehab and some we wholesale.

Rehabbing

This is the popular part of the business. There are now TV shows, such as "Flip that House" based on this technique and many people feel it is exciting. It is true that it is really fun to take something ugly and make it beautiful, but it is also the biggest headache and the riskiest of the 3 approaches. Rehabbing can also represent the biggest profit potential so I guess the risk/reward (and headache) pay off is appropriate.

Contractors

One of the biggest headaches is working with contractors and this is an area where if you are not careful, you can lose a lot of money. I have seen some investors who get around the contractor problem by doing the work themselves, but this usually doesn't last long as they realize that trading their time for contractor's wages is not in the best interest of the business.

Contractors are small businesses, and all small businesses need money. It is not unusual for a contractor to want 50% up front, another 30% in draws during, and 20% upon completion. What happens in these scenarios is that the contractor runs out of money and has a job he hasn't finished, he uses the first half of your draw to finish his last project and to buy only a few materials for yours. You see a little bit of activity and then they are off the project while finishing the other job. When they finally get back to yours they have very little of the money that was completed from the last job, but it doesn't last. Then they are gone again until they find another project to collect the initial deposit on, so they can use someone else's money to finish your job.

The answer is to find a contractor who you can pay for work completed. I let my contractors bill me on Wednesday, then I inspect on Thursday, and pay on Friday. These will not be the cheapest contractors, but they will be some of the better ones, as they have the financial resources to purchase their own materials.

Another answer is to use a good contract (yours, not their bid sheet) that outlines when they will start, be completed, and penalties for both being late and not having anyone on the job. In the contract, require necessary permits, licenses, and check their insurance.

Options, wraps, and others

Options and wraps represent a fairly broad category of investment activity which consist of various blends. Many of the techniques are somewhat advanced and may carry added risk to the novice investor. My suggestion is, as always, to get as much education as possible, and discuss various strategies with a good real estate attorney.

This portion of the business can often be the most profitable in terms of deal volume. Normally the properties involved in these "creative" financing methods are nice homes not in need of repair, just in need of a solution. Due to where the economy has been for the last 8 or so years, the majority of homes bought don't have enough equity to sell through traditional methods. Because the market has been fairly flat and in some cases still down, home owners who put a minimum down payment on their homes don't have the 10% equity it takes to sell a home. With closing costs and commission it takes about 10% for most people to sell. These strategies essentially match up the thousands of un-sellable homes with the thousands of buyers who can't get loans.

The state of the mortgage industry is such that decent homebuyers are still struggling to get loans. Necessary credit scores and underwriting guidelines have gotten fairly strict, due to fear of regulation and government reprisal. What was once considered a golden credit score is now the minimum acceptable. Many people who may have lost businesses or houses in the collapse are back on their feet with a new business and need the status of a home. Also regardless of how poorly we have run the economy, there is no stopping the march of mankind and the formation of new families, many of whom want to raise their children in their own home.

So we have somewhat of a "Perfect Storm" for these creative strategies that help people get into homes without having to get a loan in the current market.

Options

An option on a property gives you the right to purchase the property at a future date. Many investors will tie up a property with an option and then sell the option to a new buyer. When this is combined with a lease, which will make the payments for the seller, this can be packaged to a new buyer for several years until they have the ability to refinance when borrowing is easier. Option money is usually involved as a portion of the profits to the investor.

The benefits of this strategy are that it is extremely easy to find lease option buyers and that can happen in weeks instead of months. Another benefit is that they make excellent tenants, as option buyers are typically responsible for any and all repairs and will often actually improve the property.

The down side is that lease option buyers rarely improve their credit situation and typically can't buy at the end of the option period. This can lead to hard feelings for both the buyer and the old seller. There can also be issues with the option deposit (talk to an attorney) as it typically should be forfeited by the buyer but many people don't understand this and will try to get it back. This is one of the reasons that here in Texas they have put a lot of teeth in the laws regarding lease options and "executory contracts". If you are in Texas please get educated on this before entering any option period beyond 18 months!

Wraps

I remember my first Broker, sitting with her MLS book (multiple listing book, yes it was a book before computers) going through it, and calculating the difference between the loan amount and sales price of the properties to see how much down payment someone would need to purchase the property. If someone did not have enough money to outright assume the loan, they could negotiate a second loan, and sometimes these loans would be wrapped together.

This was back when many loans were assumable, I think it was in the 1980's when FHA and VA started putting a due on sale clause in their loans. In almost all loans today the due on sale clause makes the loan due whenever there is a transfer of tile. Makes sense from a lenders stand point. So how can loans be assumed today? Many home buyers, sellers, and investors are doing this today.

As the Ron White joke goes upon his arrest, "I had the right to remain silent...but I didn't have the ability."

Most lenders don't currently have the resources to know if a transfer has happened. In fact, most don't want any more foreclosed homes. It is not their business and they lose tons of money on a foreclosure. Most are happy with the payments regardless of who is making it. I know of one attorney who writes on the check when he brings a loan, that cashing the check waives their right to call the loan. He says he has never had a problem. So once again the down side of this technique is when things go sour, people stop making payments and banks want to foreclose etc. There is risk to the investor caught in the middle, an attorney can help guide on the risks.

The blended business

As I said earlier, a good business model is to use the fast cash flow generating activities of real estate to help fund and support the slower long term wealth building activities in a blended business model. One of my first mentors told me not to keep a rental unit until you could write a check for $25,000. At the time I didn't heed the advice and learned a hard lesson. Now we are careful to have both cash reserves and cash flow to help cover. Right now we target cash flow coverage at around 25%, meaning we could cover the cash needs of our properties if 25% of them were vacant.

These built in reserves of cash flow help to protect from down turns and other risks that can topple an investment portfolio if totally leveraged on cash flow. The majority of small portfolios, I see don't cash flow, let alone have excess to help off set risk. This should be a major strategy of a successful investor who is planning to hold onto investments.

Benjamin Graham, one of Warren Buffets early mentors' first rules of creating wealth was to "never ever lose money." Having a well rounded business that spins off excess cash flow is one of the best hedges against problems and surprises. Cash can solve a lot of problems.

Chapter 6
Multifamily

Which is the better real estate investment? Multifamily or single family properties?

Multifamily properties, hands down, will out perform a single family home for several reasons. First of all, having multiple units under one roof, on one site, lowers the cost to produce and maintain. They are also easier to manage as the tenants are all in one location. The more units there are, the less expensive it is to manage. At 100+ units, you are able to have most of the management and maintenance on site.

The main reason why multifamily properties out perform single family properties is that profits are built into the price of the property. Single family homes, on the other hand, are competing with owner occupant buyers who are looking at the properties for the enjoyment of living in them. I call this the "Aesthetic Value." Analyzing most single family home purchase prices, even if a large 20% down payment is made, won't produce cash flow.

True cash flow is not just what is left of the rent payment after the mortgage payment. As we saw when we looked at analyzing the single family residential property, most single family investors don't account for many of the expenses of ownership.

Multifamily real estate is bought by investors, who actually price the amount they will pay by how much they make off the property. The more sophisticated the investor, the closer they analyze the performance of a property. The formulas, ratios, and models used by investors are geared to build in their profits. The pool of potential buyers of multifamily properties all expect pricing that will allow profit.

There are arguments that single family management might be easier, and that it is usually easier to sell a single family home than an apartment or quadruplex. That may be true, but from a financial standpoint, multifamily usually out shines single family.

Just as most businesses, real estate and multifamily properties in particular, make more economic sense as the volume gets larger. Starting with small 2 to 4 family units. The more units under one roof you have the cheaper the cost and maintenance. As the unit count grows, you begin to get savings in management costs. At around 100 units, an on site manager becomes affordable and at around 150 full time maintenance becomes an option.

Risk also is reduced with the number of units. With a single family home, if it is vacant the owner must carry the whole load on the mortgage payment. With multifamily if one unit is vacant there are several other tenants that can help to cover the cost.

Another benefit of larger multifamily units is that it makes purchasing in other markets more sensible. If purchasing small units, it makes traveling to locations other than the city you live in a burden. However, if you have multiple larger number of units in one location, the financial reasons for travel can prove itself beneficial. Because all cities are not the same in terms of real estate demand, with a little bit of research you will find that many areas of the country are experiencing real estate booms fueled by job growth. These emerging markets will create great cash flow and appreciation potentially far above the returns often available in your local market.

Normally this is the next step in the investor's journey, to venture out beyond their local markets. Whether utilizing a well qualified to team to find, analyze, acquire, repair, and manage the property, or through a syndication, the returns to having successfully recognized and invested in an emerging market has been key to quite a few fortunes.

Finding the emerging market

As stated before, jobs are what drive demand for real estate. So a local government that has a pro business outlook and has successfully brought in new companies is a good place to look first.

The niche analysis

The emerging market is that market where demand has just begun to switch from oversupply in what is a buyers market to more demand than supply in a sellers market.

Fueled by job growth, this analysis looks at new job growth and new population and compares that to the number of rental units available to determine the shortage. Then research is done on how many new units are on the books for development. When after considering the new developments, there remains a substantial shortage, here is the opportunity.

As of this writing, there are several areas around the country where job growth is heating up demand in the rental market. The Texas and Dakota oil businesses have quite a few cities starving for places to rent. Medical technology companies serving the aging population have created technology campuses in cities like San Antonio and Dallas with a demand of mid scale properties.

Another good aspect for the emerging market is that the city not be too small, 100,000 population at minimum for overall stability. International airports, colleges and military bases, are all important.

Hindrance to new development is important for appreciation, as demand is not filled with new properties and rents rise. As rents rise, so do values. No land available for development is a hindrance, as is construction costs that are too high, or anti development sentiment and high infrastructure fees by a city. These all dampen the returns to new development of properties.

Discussing emerging markets and investing outside of your city is not to mean in any way that the investor should not invest in multifamily in their own city, far from it. Management and supervision in your own city is much easier and market feel and area is more easily obtained. Care should be taken to ensure sufficient cash flow for the property to perform, regardless of what the market is doing in your city.

Chapter 7
Analysis of the Multifamily

As we will be discussing financial matters, I am not a CPA. Everyone's financial situation is different and you should always consult your financial counselor before making any decisions. I am, however, a Broker and an Appraiser. The following are some of my observations regarding multifamily properties.

In the shifting economic sands of the coming years, it will be risky to speculate in multifamily properties. Meaning, that you buy the property at full market value and hope that appreciation makes you money. As was discussed about single family homes, the goal of the successful "New Market" Investor is to move from speculating in real estate to true investing, where the money is made in the original purchase.

This requires the new market investor to find a value play, a problem in a property to be solved. Here are the main six value plays to look for:

Burnt out landlords
These owners are flat tired of dealing with their properties, whether through lack of management skills and tools, lack of energy, or better opportunities elsewhere, these owners need help getting out!

Poor management
Bad management will show in many different areas, maintenance not done, bad debt collection, high vacancies, low rents, all symptoms of poor management and all are opportunities to make a good deal on a property, correct the problems and make money.

Properties that need repair
It is not unusual for an owner to take the money out of a property and not do repairs. Lack of repairs will cause high vacancies as tenants leave, and low rents. Curing these problems usually has a positive effect on cash flow.

Low rents
Whether through lazy management, fear of tenant loss, or just being unaware of what market rents really are, some properties can be bought, Rents raised, and value raised immediately.

High vacancies
Higher than market vacancies are a sign typically of poor marketing, management, or one of the other factors listed above. Find these properties, find the issue and solve the issue for the profits entitled to the true investor willing to spend the time and effort to purchase properties with built in profits!

For example, lets assume that a 100 unit property has 100,000 yearly cash flow and is purchased for $1,000,000 and the going capitalization rate (cap rate, we will look more closely at later) is 10%. The owner solving one of the above problems and is able to increase monthly rents by just $25 per month, has increased the cash flow by $30,000 (25 x 100) x 12. At a 10% cap rate that $30,000 increase in revenue increases the value of the property to $1,300,000. $300,000 for knowing what problem to solve, not bad! Again we will look at cap rates shortly but I wanted to make this point about finding properties with built in profits.

All properties are different, but all investors are essentially after the same thing, cash flow. So the ability to find some type of indicator to represent the amount of cash flow from the property is necessary for investors to compare and communicate the performance of the property. We will look at some of the issues regarding this. To begin lets look at the different property classifications.

Types of properties

Multifamily properties are often given a letter classification to categorize in terms of quality, location and desirability of the property. Type "A" properties are top quality, usually fairly new built within last 10 years. They are in desirable locations usually in the path of progress (where the city is growing). These properties sell for more as they have a longer economic life. There are more luxury cars in the parking lots of these apartments.

Type "B" properties are typically white collar by nature, in OK areas and were built in the last 20 Years. Late model sedans and minivans are in these parking lots.

Type "C" properties are more blue collar and are in marginal areas. Built in the last 30 years, these properties have more work trucks and older model cars in the parking lots. Section 8 housing is typically in these.

Type "D" properties are in the war zones. Over 50 years old these properties have functional problems and tenant problems. Most investors should stay away from properties in these areas as they represent very special management skills.

We make the most money in the B properties verging on the A areas, or the C properties also in the path of progress that can be repositioned to a B property.

Analyzing the cash flow

Income

Starting with the income, we will look at the actual income of the property. Most sellers and Realtors will present you with a "pro-forma" income statement for a property that shows the income if 100% rented. The problem with this is that the property is not 100% rented and that the vacant units represent work that the seller did not do but that you will have to. Why pay someone for work that they did not do? The difference represents problems they were unable to solve. We don't analyze on pro forma revenues! We pay only for actual cash flow on properties. We must get the actual numbers from the owner to analyze revenue.

Market rents VS current rents

Market rents can be determined by looking at what similar properties are leasing for. Current rents are what is being charged. The difference is a value play but the initial analysis is always performed on what is actually happening on the property, so the value is calculated on current rents only, never market rents.

Expenses

Vacancy and credit loss
Use actual vacancy numbers or 10% vacancy rates for initial analysis purposes. Many investors use 5%, but the conservative investor will find value and profits driven to their bottom lines.

Management fees
Whether you plan to manage the property yourself or not, you need to make calculate the cost of management and subtract that from the income, otherwise you will pay the seller for the work you will do. Typically 8% to 10% on smaller properties and 5% to 8 % on larger.

Repairs and maintenance
Average repairs and maintenance run 10% of gross annual income. Many sellers claim they have none of these expenses which actually means there will be a lot of repairs and maintenance to do.

Operating expenses

What you, the owner, will take out of your pocket and pay.
1. Real Estate Taxes
2. Insurance
3. Water and Sewer
4. Snow Removal
5. Any Utilities
6. Trash Removal
7. Legal

Processing the cash flow
For your initial screening, estimates will suffice, however, during your due diligence period on the property make certain that you look at the details behind all of the numbers with the seller. It is not necessary for me to mention that many sellers will try to hide expenses from you.

After confirming the cash flow from rents, and subtracting out vacancy and credit loss, we have the Gross Operating Income or GOI.

After subtracting the other expenses, we come to the Net Operating Income or NOI.

After subtracting the debt service, we have cash flow before Taxes or CFBT.

Determining Price

Price as it relates to a multifamily income property is determined by the income. What will an investor pay for the cash flow? So some type of indicated is necessary to reflect the relationship between price and cash flow. One of the most used is the Capitalization Rate or Cap Rate.

1. Cap rate = Net Operating Income/Vale (price of the property)

So if you know any 2 variables in the formula, you can solve for the 3rd

2. Net Operating Income = Value (selling price) X Cap Rate

3. Value (selling price) = Net Operating Income/Cap Rate

So at this point we will be using the 3rd variation of the formula. $75,000 NOI at an 11% cap rate would indicate a value of $681,818.

Cap rates usually range between 8% and 12%, and it has an inverse relation to the value. The higher the Cap Rate, the lower the value, and the lower the Cap Rate the higher the value.

"A" Type properties usually have the lowest cap rates usually around 7%, next lowest are "B" properties usually 8% to 9%. "C" Properties usually sell for 10% to 11% with "D" properties selling at 12% or higher.

Cash on cash return

This performance indicator is one the most revealing. The Cash on Cash return tells you that for every dollar that you took out of your pocket to get into the deal, how much of that dollar you will get back at the end of the first year. This indicates how quickly you get your money back.

Here is the formula:

$$\frac{\text{Cash flow (Net Operating Income} - \text{Debt Service)}}{\text{Acquisition Costs (Down Payment + any money needed for deal)}}$$

You should be looking for Cash on Cash return for 14% to 20%. Which means you will be getting 14 to 20 cents back of every dollar put in.

Return on investment

$$\frac{\text{NOI} - \text{Debt Service} + \text{Principal Reduction}}{\text{Acquisition Costs}}$$

This calculation is a little more complicated at principal reduction calculation requires the financial function of a calculator or computer to determine principal payback. It does, however allow you to compare a particular real estate investment with others, like stocks, to determine which has the highest return.

Debt coverage ratio

This ratio is looked at by lenders to determine the ability of the property to service the debt.

$$\frac{\text{NOI}}{\text{Debt service}}$$

1.3 or more is usually needed to support a lending decision on a property.

So the target financials for the conservative New Market Investors will be a package representing a soundly performing property, able to generate cash flow in various market cycles. These targets would be a cap rate of 10% to 12%, a Cash on Cash return of 15%, and a debt coverage ratio of 1.3 or better. Valuation indicators coupled with a value play on the property should help to ensure sound performance.

Becoming a new market investor

As we discussed earlier, one of the key things to becoming a successful new market investor is to have better tools available and a realistic analysis. The new market investor must have the ability to analyze properties appropriately, making it account for as many of the variables in income and expenses as possible. They must also be able to price their purchase to guarantee or dial-in returns when the property is purchased. This requires the new market investor to have an understanding of the best way to analyze properties with an understanding of what the cost components are as well as the other variables that kidnap and eat up profits.

The second thing necessary for the new market investor is a willingness and ability to go the extra mile both in analysis and fighting properties. Much of the success for the new market investor will be the ability to have enough potential properties to view and analyze so that they don't feel the need to take marginal properties into their portfolio. This requires better marketing techniques and the ability to find and analyze more properties in a volume typesetting.

Next steps

There are various ways that a person can get more information on investing and continue their education to grow their understanding. This book is certainly one of them. There are also home study courses available on our website, **newmarketinvestor.com**.

For those who understand the value of coaching and mentoring, and how both can increase profits and shorten learning time, we have personal mentoring available.

www.ingramcontent.com/pod-product-compliance
Lightning Source LLC
Chambersburg PA
CBHW071826170526
45167CB00003B/1435